I WITNESS WAR

THE WAR AGAINST ISIS

ANGELA ADAMS

Cavendish
Square

New York

Published in 2018 by Cavendish Square Publishing, LLC
243 5th Avenue, Suite 136, New York, NY 10016

First Edition

Website: cavendishsq.com

This publication represents the opinions and views of the author based on his or her personal experience, knowledge, and research. The information in this book serves as a general guide only. The author and publisher have used their best efforts in preparing this book and disclaim liability rising directly or indirectly from the use and application of this book.

All websites were available and accurate when this book was sent to press.

Library of Congress Cataloging-in-Publication Data

Names: McNiven, Lauren.
Title: The war against ISIS / Lauren McNiven.
Description: New York : Cavendish Square, 2018. | Series: I witness war | Includes bibliographical references and index. | Audience: Grades 5–8.
Identifiers: ISBN 9781502632562 (library bound) | | ISBN 9781502634337 (pbk.) | ISBN 9781502632555 (ebook)
Subjects: LCSH: IS (Organization)—Juvenile literature.
Classification: LCC HV6433.I722 A33 2018 | DDC 956.054—dc23

Produced for Cavendish Square by Calcium
Editors: Sarah Eason and Jennifer Sanderson
Designers: Paul Myerscough and Simon Borrough
Picture Researcher: Rachel Blount

Printed in the United States of America

CONTENTS

CHAPTER 1

BLACK FLAGS RISE

ISIS is an extremist Muslim group. ISIS stands for the Islamic State in Iraq and Syria, the two countries where ISIS is most active. The group is also known as the Islamic State (IS) and the Islamic State in Iraq and the Levant (ISIL). "The Levant" is a term used to describe a geographic region made up of countries that border the eastern Mediterranean Sea, stretching from Greece to Egypt. "Daesh" is another name for ISIS. It is an acronym for the group's name in Arabic.

A terrorist is a person or organization that uses violence and acts of terror, and the fear these acts creates, to achieve a goal. The Global Terrorism Index is a measure that ranks countries that are most affected by terrorism. In 2015, Iraq was ranked first, and Syria was ranked fifth. It was in these two countries that ISIS rose to power. Over a few short years, ISIS has extended its reach beyond the Middle East. Victims of its campaign of terror are found all over the world, turning the war against ISIS into a global war that affects people of all faiths, races, genders, and backgrounds. To understand how ISIS rose to power, it is important to understand what was happening in Syria and Iraq when the organization formed.

For decades, many Middle Eastern countries have experienced conflict. The Iraq War (2003–2011) left Iraq unstable after the removal of the country's **dictator**, Saddam Hussein. In 2011, **civil war** broke out in Syria, to the west of Iraq. Amid the fighting in both countries, the black flag of ISIS rose as the group gained power, territory, and followers.

The black flag of ISIS flies over the city of Azaz in Syria.

ISIS is known to operate in many Middle Eastern countries, including Syria, Iraq, Saudi Arabia, Egypt, and Yemen.

The ultimate goal of ISIS is to establish a global caliphate. A caliphate is a state that is governed by the group's extreme interpretation of laws set out in the Koran, the holy book of Islam. ISIS views anyone who opposes the establishment of its caliphate, or who does not share its extremist beliefs, as an enemy. In June 2014, in Mosul, Iraq, the ISIS caliph, or leader, Abu Bakr al-Baghdadi, officially declared the establishment of an Islamic state. This newly established state covered the territory controlled by ISIS that straddles the Syrian-Iraqi border.

Islam is an ancient religion that shares its roots with Christianity and Judaism. It is practiced by more than 1.6 billion people around the world. Muslims believe in the teachings of the prophet Muhammad, and they worship Allah, the Arabic word for "God." The two main sects, or branches, of Islam are Sunni and Shia. The divide between these two branches occurred thousands of years ago, following the death of Muhammad in 632 CE. After his passing, Muslims disagreed over who should be their new leader. Two groups formed, who later became known as the Sunnites and the Shiites. The Sunnites wanted the caliph to be chosen by the Muslim community, while the Shiites wanted the leader to be a descendant of Muhammad.

The Sunnites won the battle, and Abu Bakr, a close companion of Muhammad, became the first caliph. Over hundreds of years, the divide between the Shia and Sunni shifted. It became less about religion and more about power.

In Iraq, about 60 percent of people are Shia, and 32 percent are Sunni. For more than twenty years, a Sunni government led by Saddam Hussein controlled the country. The majority Shia were oppressed and persecuted. In Iraq, ISIS found a foothold in areas dominated by Sunni. In Syria, 74 percent of people are Sunni, and 13 percent are Shia. Syrian president Bashar al-Assad and many of his top officials are Shia. During the early months of the Syrian civil war, ISIS positioned itself as an ally of

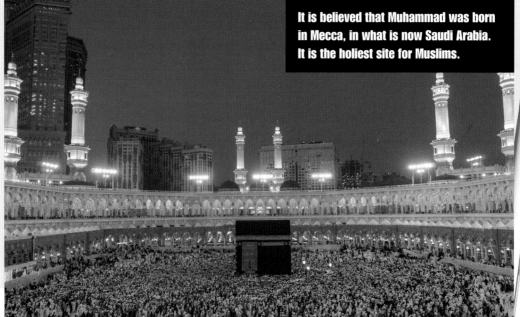

It is believed that Muhammad was born in Mecca, in what is now Saudi Arabia. It is the holiest site for Muslims.

the people, fighting the al-Assad regime. This is one way they gained power in places such as Raqqa, in northeastern Syria.

ISIS's interpretation of Islam is extreme. It considers the Sunni branch to be the "pure" form of Islam. It views Shia Muslims as apostates, or people who have abandoned their religion. ISIS **militants** are also called jihadists.

A jihad is a fight against those who oppose or are enemies of Islam. Sometimes a jihad is also called a holy war. The word can also be used to describe someone's struggle to be a good Muslim. In the case of ISIS, its members are jihadists because they are at war with those who do not share their interpretation of Islam. Today, "jihad" has a negative meaning because of terrorist groups such as ISIS.

The white writing on the top of the ISIS flag reads, "There is no God but Allah. Muhammad is the messenger of Allah." The black writing in the white circle below reads, "Muhammad is the messenger of God."

In 2004, ISIS was founded in Iraq as a branch of al-Qaeda—the organization responsible for the September 11, 2001, terrorist attacks against the United States. At that time, ISIS was known as al-Qaeda in Iraq (AQI). Under the leadership of Abu Musab al-Zarqawi, AQI launched attacks against the Iraqi government, which was made up of many Shia Muslims. In 2006, al-Zarqawi was killed in an air strike. An Egyptian named Abu Ayyub al-Masri took over and changed the organization's name to the Islamic State in Iraq (ISI). Over the next four years, the group weakened, until 2010, when Jordanian Abu Bakr al-Baghdadi became the new leader. In 2004, al-Baghdadi had been a prisoner at Camp Bucca, a US-run detention center in southern Iraq. It was at Camp Bucca that the ideology of ISIS, as it is understood today, began to catch on with jihadists.

In 2011, civil war broke out in Syria after the government attacked **civilians** who had been protesting peacefully for democracy. The government army, led by President Bashar al-Assad, began fighting rebel forces. As the war dragged on, the rebels weakened, all while ISIS was gaining power. In April 2013, al-Baghdadi announced that ISI was combining forces with the Nusra Front, another terrorist group, to form the Islamic State in Iraq and the Levant (ISIL). The Nusra Front rejected the union. By early 2014, ISIS had broken away from al-Qaeda and had also taken control of the northeastern city of Raqqa from the Syrian rebels.

Guards patrol Camp Bucca, which during the Iraq War housed thousands of prisoners, including al-Baghdadi.

I WITNESS WAR

Raqqa is the self-proclaimed capital of the caliphate. In the excerpt below, an ISIS **defector** explains how ISIS (Daesh) seized the city in 2013:

Before the ISIS occupation, the population of Raqqa was about 260,000.

"When Daesh came to Raqqa, Jaysh al-Hur [the Free Syrian Army] was in power, but Daesh took over for many reasons. First, Daesh sent small groups to establish themselves inside the city. Secondly, they sent suicide bombers of young boys, especially to the gates where Jaysh al-Hur had guards. This was very effective, as everyone feared the suicide bombers, and it was very difficult to distinguish if an approaching child was a suicide bomber or not. Being unwilling to shoot a possibly innocent child, the sentries would run away, and Daesh could enter. Lastly, Jaysh al-Hur began to realize it was too late to fight against Daesh—because they had established themselves by using cells already inside the city, who began to explode things. So Jaysh al-Hur fighters left with hardly any fighting."

What does the use of children as suicide bombers suggest about ISIS?

Why do you think the rebel soldiers left Raqqa without fighting?

Research the word "cells." Why do you think a cell might be so effective as a terrorist tool?

CHAPTER 2

ESTABLISHING THE ISLAMIC STATE

After gaining a foothold in Raqqa, ISIS rose to power swiftly, taking much of the world by surprise. By February 2014, the extremists controlled the city of Fallujah in Iraq, about 40 miles (70 km) from Baghdad. By June, ISIS had captured Mosul, the second-largest city in Iraq, and Tikrit, the hometown of Saddam Hussein. From the Great Mosque in Mosul, on June 29, 2014, al-Baghdadi declared the establishment of a caliphate and renamed the group the "Islamic State (IS)."

By establishing the caliphate and declaring himself caliph, al-Baghdadi marked a new chapter in IS's reign of terror. He called on all Muslims to pledge **allegiance** to the Islamic State. The caliphate now stretched across northeastern Syria and northwestern Iraq, an area more than twice the size of Pennsylvania. IS started setting up a so-called government to run its caliphate. To maintain control, militants erected roadblocks and checkpoints.

The Great Mosque in Mosul was built hundreds of years ago by a Muslim ruler named Nur al-Din Mahmoud Zangi.

The economies of Syria and Iraq rely heavily on oil. ISIS also relies greatly on this valuable resource.

This made it nearly impossible for people and material goods to pass in or out of a city. Items such as food, medicine, and fuel become difficult to find. For the families being held captive, it became difficult to meet basic needs. Laws were introduced that forced young men to join IS as soldiers. A police force, called the *hisbah*, roamed the streets, punishing anyone seen breaking the laws set out by IS. Schools were set up where people were brainwashed to adopt IS's extreme interpretation of Islam. Children were especially targeted. Young boys were sent to schools where they studied religion, then they were sent to camps where they were trained as soldiers. These boys are known as "cubs of the caliphate."

The area under IS control included many oil fields, a resource that is highly prized in the Middle East. The militants have fought to take over places where oil is plentiful to fund their campaign of terror. The militants sell this valuable resource on the **black market**. During the summer of 2014, experts estimated that IS was earning $3 million a day through oil sales. The oil is sold in IS-controlled areas and is also smuggled to nearby countries, such as Turkey, where it is sold at a lower price.

In March 2015, the International Committee of the Red Cross estimated that ten million people lived in areas under ISIS control. The innocent people trapped in these areas were forced to live under sharia law, which are strict laws based on the Koran and other Islamic teachings. Sharia laws were written during the 700s and 800s CE by Muslim rulers. ISIS believes that sharia law must apply to all parts of a person's life, such as how a person prays, eats, and dresses. This is the system of law used in the caliphate. ISIS militants read the Koran and other Islamic teachings and take

them literally. They twist sharia to "allow" them the power to punish civilians in brutal ways and to do so in the name of Allah. Harsh punishments, including beheadings, lashings, **crucifixions**, and stonings, are carried out in public. These are just some of the many ways that ISIS uses fear to control the people trapped in the caliphate. Images of people being punished are also used to spread fear and to **recruit** fighters to join ISIS in its war.

The Koran teaches that there is only one God, Allah. ISIS militants believe that anyone who worships multiple gods, or a false god, is an enemy who can be punished according to sharia law.

While some women in different countries choose to wear a niqab for their personal faith, in ISIS-controlled areas, it is a symbol of oppression.

Women must abide by even stricter laws. ISIS does not allow women to be alone in public. They must always be with their husbands or a male relative. ISIS also restricts the health care of women. It is forbidden for male doctors to be alone with women. ISIS militants dictate that all women must always wear a full **niqab**, which means that their entire body, including their hair, face, and feet, must be covered whenever they are outside of their home. ISIS wants the niqabs to be black, without color, and sometimes even demand that young girls' hair be covered, too, with a **hijab**. If a woman is seen outside without the full niqab, she can be beaten and fined. Men can be punished, too, if the women they are escorting are not following the strict dress code. Many women stay at home to avoid being punished by ISIS militants.

13

The war against ISIS, alongside the ongoing violence in Iraq and Syria, has forced millions of people from their homes. When people flee their homes but remain in the country, they are known as internally displaced persons (IDPs). People who escape to safety in another country are called refugees. Many victims of the war against ISIS live in camps set up by **humanitarian** organizations such as the United Nations High Commissioner for Refugees (UNHCR) and the Red Cross. Recent statistics show that almost five million people have left Syria and are living in nearby countries such as Turkey, Lebanon, and Jordan. Nearly 300 thousand refugees have fled Iraq. Some people escaping ISIS have made their way to countries in Europe, as well as Canada and the United States. By early 2017, there were still more than six million people internally displaced in Syria, and more than three million people were displaced in Iraq.

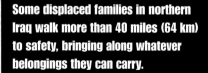

Some displaced families in northern Iraq walk more than 40 miles (64 km) to safety, bringing along whatever belongings they can carry.

I WITNESS WAR

The Zelican camp in northern Iraq provides food and shelter for many people who have been displaced by the recent fighting in Mosul and the surrounding area. In the camp, an organization called World Vision set up a space where children can draw pictures. Fourteen-year-old Hamaad, who used this name to protect his identity, recalls an ISIS attack in his neighborhood in Mosul:

"We had a very big, beautiful house. We also had a big garden where we had animals and lots [of] trees. A remote-controlled plane struck my neighbor's house, and it was very strong—the sound was like 'whoosh.' Five people died, and the rest were hurt. I thought, 'Now it's going to hit us!' I was scared by that bad plane. We were all terrified. I want to be a doctor and specialize in pediatrics."

Why do you think Hamaad has to use a different name to share his story?

What words would you use to describe an explosion? Why do you think Hamaad uses the word "whoosh"?

What do you think Hamaad is describing when he says "remote-controlled plane"?

15

CHAPTER 3

LIVING IN TERROR

After capturing Mosul in 2014, ISIS continued to expand its territory. The group's military capacity was strengthened when it seized tanks and other weapons abandoned by the retreating (fleeing) Iraqi army. Soon, ISIS turned north and began launching attacks on Iraqi Kurdistan.

Kurdistan is a mountainous region that covers parts of eastern Turkey, northern Iraq, western Iran, and northern Syria and Armenia. It is the homeland of about twenty-five million Kurds, a distinct ethnic group with its own language and culture. For hundreds of years, the Kurds have fought to establish their own country. Many Middle Eastern countries, such as Syria and Iraq, do not support this idea. In Iraq, Kurdistan is recognized as an **autonomous** region. It has its own military called the Peshmerga, which means "those who face death." The Peshmerga, known as fierce soldiers, fought to protect their homeland but struggled to push back against the ISIS advance.

Iraq and Iran are the only countries in the Middle East that recognize Kurdistan as a distinct region within their borders.

Two Peshmerga soldiers patrol near Mosul, the largest city under IS control.

As ISIS moved farther north, more towns fell under its rule. Tens of thousands of people fled. When ISIS gained control of a new town, it quickly destroyed holy sites that it considered heretical (against their religious beliefs). Crosses were toppled from Christian churches, shrines were bombed, and religious texts were burned. In Mosul, Jonah's Tomb, a holy site for both Christian and Muslims, was rigged with explosives. In a single blast, the towering structure was reduced to a pile of rubble. The militants also turned their attention to persecuting religious minorities living in the Kurdish region. In early August, ISIS captured the city of Qaraqosh, which was home to the largest Christian population in Iraq. Christians were given three choices: convert to Islam, pay a tax called *jiyza*, or leave. The same choice was offered to Christians in the occupied city of Mosul. Muslims living in the region were also targeted by ISIS. On its bloody campaign, ISIS soldiers executed more than 1,500 Shia soldiers at an army base in Tikrit in June. In August, more than seven hundred members of the Sheitat tribe were slaughtered in eastern Syria for fighting against ISIS.

On August 3, 2014, ISIS seized the city of Sinjar, which is home to many Yazidis, a Kurdish-speaking ethnic group. The Yazidi live mainly in northwest Iraq. Their ancient belief system blends elements of Islam, Christianity, and **Zoroastrianism**, a 3,500-year-old religion. The Yazidi faith is complex and often misunderstood. One of the Yazidi main deities, or gods, is called Malak Taus. Another name for Malak Taus is Shaytan, the Arabic word for "devil." As a result of the translation of Shaytan, the Yazidi have been labeled and persecuted by ISIS as "devil-worshipers." This small group, which accounts for fewer than 2 percent of Iraq's total population, has suffered greatly at the hands of the extremists.

As ISIS militants began to round up the Yazidis in the Sinjar area, hundreds of terrified families fled into the nearby mountains. Not everyone was able to escape.

Yazidi children receive aid at a camp in Kurdistan.

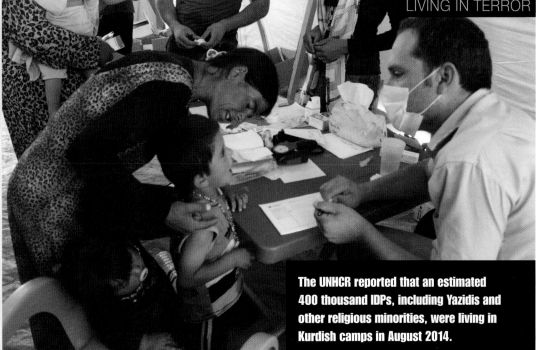

The UNHCR reported that an estimated 400 thousand IDPs, including Yazidis and other religious minorities, were living in Kurdish camps in August 2014.

In Sinjar and the surrounding area, ISIS massacred more than five thousand Yazidi men and captured many more. The men were forced to convert to Islam or be killed. The Yazidi women and girls were kidnapped and taken away as slaves. Young Yazidi boys had to convert and join ISIS as soldiers. An estimated 200 thousand Yazidis were trapped in the hot, dry mountains without food or water. The Iraqi government reached out to the US government for help to rescue the innocent people stuck above Sinjar, and on August 8, US President Barack Obama ordered the first air strikes to be carried out on ISIS targets in northern Iraq.

Humanitarian aid was air-dropped in the mountains above Sinjar. On the ground, the Peshmerga came to the rescue, opening a path for Yazidis to escape down the mountain. The Kurdish regional government set up camps for the displaced Yazidi.

The United Nations (UN) has labeled the ISIS persecution of the Yazidi and other religious minorities as a genocide. A genocide is the deliberate killing of a specific group of people based on their race, religion, or sexual orientation. More than thirty mass graves (graves for multiple remains) have been found on the mountain in areas recaptured from ISIS.

19

The imprisoned Yazidi women and girls from the Sinjar area were sent to the caliphate. The captives become *sabaya*, meaning "slave," to ISIS, and are taken to markets where they are bought and sold like livestock. They are locked up, beaten, and **raped** by their captors. Some ISIS soldiers also force the women to convert to Islam. The militants believe that the Koran grants them permission to rape women who are not Muslim, and that by doing so, it will bring them closer to Allah. ISIS also uses this sex trade of women and girls as a tool for recruiting soldiers. They are promised "wives" if they join ISIS. Women can be forced to marry several jihadists and are passed from one militant to another as "gifts."

Some Yazidi women are able to escape. They make contact with their families and are smuggled to safety. Other families pay thousands of dollars as a **ransom** to free their imprisoned family members. In 2016, the UN reported that 3,200 Yazidi women were still being held captive in cities such as Mosul and Raqqa.

In August 2014, a rally in Paris, France, is held to show support and raise awareness for the Yazidis and Kurds being persecuted by ISIS.

I WITNESS WAR

The Liberation of Christian and Yazidi Children of Iraq (CYCI) is a Canadian-based charity. It helps fund the rescue of Yazidi women who are enslaved by ISIS. Nihad is a young Yazidi survivor. Her family was captured in Sinjar on August 3, 2014. She escaped from the caliphate with the help of CYCI. Today, she has returned to Kurdistan. In an interview, Nihad describes daily life as a sabaya, being passed from one ISIS militant to another:

Many Yazidi women who escape captivity rely on aid to help them recover from their past.

"Every day, they abused us, we were hit for being Yazidi. They forced us to practice Islam. I was sixteen years old at the time. I stayed with that man for about one-and-a-half months, and then that man was killed in Syria … I tried to escape the house and find my family, but I was caught near Kirkuk. When I was captured near Kirkuk, they took me to another leader from Mosul."

How would you feel if you were forced to practice a religion that was against your beliefs?

Why do you think Nihad decided to share her story?

Why do you think IS moves Yazidi women from one city to another?

21

CHAPTER 4

OPERATION INHERENT RESOLVE

The first US air strikes marked a definite turning point in the war against ISIS. In September 2014, several countries joined together to form the Global **Coalition** against Daesh. Members include Western countries, such as the United States, Canada, and the United Kingdom (UK), as well as Middle Eastern countries, such as Jordan and Iraq. By 2017, sixty-eight countries had joined the US-led Coalition.

The Global Coalition set out five strategies to stop ISIS. Some Coalition members provide military support to soldiers on the front lines by supplying weapons and training. In Iraq, the Coalition has trained more than sixty-five thousand fighters. Many countries, such as the United States, France, and the UK, also participate in air strike attacks on ISIS targets. By March 2017, more than eleven thousand air strikes had been carried out in Iraq. More than seven thousand had taken place in Syria. Member countries have strengthened security measures to stop people from traveling to

The US military has carried out the highest number of air strikes against IS targets. By March 2017, US forces had conducted almost fifteen thousand hits in Syria and Iraq.

The ruins of the ancient city of Palmyra have stood for more than four thousand years. Many priceless treasures have been looted from this cultural site.

Syria and Iraq to join ISIS. Military forces have also worked to control the border between Syria and Turkey, where thousands of jihadists have crossed to join ISIS.

The Middle East is rich in oil. ISIS controls oil fields in Iraq and Syria, and uses profits from the sale of this resource to fund its campaign of terror. At one time, ISIS controlled 60 percent of oil fields in Syria and 5 percent in Iraq. The Coalition has led air strikes against ISIS-controlled oil fields and also imposed international **sanctions** to forbid countries from purchasing

oil from ISIS. ISIS has also profited from selling artifacts (man-made objects of historical significance) plundered from ancient sites, such as the ruins of Palmyra in Syria. The Coalition is working to block the sale of these treasures on the black market.

The war against ISIS has affected thousands of people living in Syria and Iraq. The Coalition works with organizations to provide food, water, shelter, medicine, and other aid to those who have been displaced by the fighting. It also works to resettle people in areas that have been liberated from ISIS.

Kobani is a city located in the Kurdish region of Syria, close to the Turkish border. The city had been under Kurdish control since July 2012 when the People's Protection Units (YPG), the militia made up of Syrian Kurds, had liberated (freed) it from the government army. In September 2014, ISIS soldiers began attacking Kobani and nearby towns. Over 170 thousand men, women, and children fled across the border as the militants closed in. Turkey now hosts an estimated 1.7 million Syrian refugees. New refugee camps were built along the border to provide food, water, and shelter for the waves of people arriving each day.

Backed by air strikes from members of the newly formed Coalition, YPG soldiers, along with rebel militias, stayed behind to fight for Kobani. In late October 2014, Kurdish forces from Iraq arrived to reinforce the fighters battling IS. By January the following year, after four months of combat, the city was completely liberated from ISIS. The victory marked an early success in the Coalition's campaign. However, more than 3,200 buildings were destroyed during the battle.

Suruc refugee camp housed more than thirty-five thousand Syrian Kurds who fled Kobani.

The first US air strikes were carried out on IS targets in Kobani on September 27, 2014.

In October 2014, the US-led military mission in Syria and Iraq received its name: Operation Inherent Resolve. The Department of Defense released a statement explaining why this name was chosen for its mission to defeat ISIS, which is referred to as ISIL below:

"The name 'Inherent Resolve' is intended to reflect the unwavering resolve and deep commitment of the US and partner nations in the region and around the globe, to eliminate the terrorist group ISIL and the threat they pose to Iraq, the region, and the wider international community. It also symbolizes the willingness and dedication of Coalition members to work closely with friends in the region and apply all available dimensions of national power necessary—diplomatic, informational, military, and economic—to degrade and ultimately destroy ISIL."

Why do you think Syria is not referred to in the statement but Iraq is? What does this reveal about the relationship between the United States and the Syrian government?

Look up the meaning of the word "resolve." Why do you think the US military chose to use this word?

"Degrade" means "to treat someone without respect." Why is this action important in the fight against ISIS?

CHAPTER 5

A GLOBAL WAR

As ISIS began to lose territory on the ground, the number of global attacks carried out and inspired by the extremists increased. Many of these acts of terror were launched in retaliation against countries that were actively fighting to destroy ISIS. Others were carried out to draw the world's attention away from the territory ISIS was losing in Iraq and Syria.

On August 19, 2014, just days after the first US air strikes, ISIS released a gruesome video showing the beheading of US journalist James Foley. Foley had been held hostage by ISIS for almost two years after being kidnapped while reporting on the Syrian civil war. In the video, ISIS soldiers warned the United States that more Americans would be killed if the air strikes continued. Over the next few months, the militants murdered more Western journalists and aid workers, including journalists Steven Sotloff and Kenji Goto, and humanitarian workers David Haines, Alan

A man lights a candle in front of the Bataclan theater in Paris, France, in memory of the victims of the November, 2015 terrorist attack.

Henning, Peter Kassig, and Kayla Mueller, as well as Japanese national Haruna Yakuna. Jordanian Moaz al-Kasasbeh was captured by ISIS after his plane crashed near Raqqa during a bombing mission in late December 2014. In February 2015, ISIS released a video that showed the pilot being burned alive. Rather than backing down, Jordan increased its air strikes against ISIS.

On November 7, 2015, ISIS launched its first major attack on a Western country. Militants armed with guns and bombs led a series of coordinated attacks at six different locations in Paris, France. Hundreds of people were wounded and 130 people died. ISIS announced that the attack was in response to French air strikes against the caliphate. Rather than pull out of the fight in the Middle East, France increased its air strikes against ISIS targets. In March 2016, ISIS struck in the Belgian capital of Brussels. Bombs were set off in the airport and subway, killing thirty-two innocent civilians and injuring many more. Belgium, which has previously pulled out of the Coalition as a result of the high financial costs, rejoined the fight in May. The world was sending a clear message to ISIS: its reign of terror was coming to an end.

Abu Bakr al-Baghdadi has called on Muslims everywhere to pledge their loyalty to ISIS. Terrorist organizations all over the world have publicly declared their allegiance to the caliph and the caliphate. Some branches have been started by jihadists who traveled to the caliphate, then returned to their home countries. Others are groups that share the same extremist ideologies and the goal of establishing a truly Islamic state. The US government has determined that ISIS has official branches in eighteen countries, spread out across North Africa, the Middle East, and Southeast Asia. The countries include Algeria, Nigeria, Libya, the Sinai Peninsula in Egypt, Saudi Arabia, Yemen, Afghanistan, Pakistan, and Russia. In 2016, Nigeria and Libya had the highest-known number of fighters loyal to the caliphate.

Boko Haram is an Islamic extremist group that has been active in Nigeria in Africa since 2002. The group also operates in neighboring countries including Chad, Cameroon, and Niger. In 2014, Boko Haram made headlines when it kidnapped more than 270 schoolgirls in Nigeria's northern province of Chibok. In March 2015, Boko Haram pledged its support to ISIS. In 2015, the group was believed to have about

In London, England, protestors gather outside the Nigerian embassy to pressure the government to rescue more than two hundred girls who were kidnapped by Boko Haram in 2014.

A US fighter jet takes off from a ship in the Mediterranean Sea. Its mission is to strike an IS target in Sirte.

fifteen thousand soldiers. That same year, the Global Terrorism Index ranked Boko Haram as the second-deadliest terror group, responsible for 5,478 documented deaths. ISIS ranked first and was responsible for 6,141 documented deaths.

ISIS gained its foothold in Syria during the uprising that led to the civil war. A similar uprising in Libya, a small country in North Africa, provided a similar footing. Three hundred people, who had fought for ISIS in Syria and Iraq,

returned to Libya and started the Youth Shura Council. In June 2014, the group announced its allegiance to IS. In June 2015, with a force of between 5,000 and 6,500 fights, it captured the coastal city of Sirte. The residents of Sirte were forced to live under strict sharia law. Many of the fighters holding the city were foreigners from places such as Syria, Iraq, and Tunisia. In August 2016, the US began air strikes on IS targets in Libya. By the end of December, ISIS had abandoned Sirte, their last **stronghold** in the country.

Homegrown terrorism is an act of terror that is committed by citizens against people in their own country. These acts are also known as lone-wolf attacks. In North America, several attacks have been carried out by Muslim extremists who have been inspired by ISIS. In April 2013, two brothers set off two homemade bombs at the Boston Marathon. Three people were killed, and more than 250 were injured. In October 2014, in Montreal, Quebec, a Muslim radical ran over two soldiers. Two days later in Ottawa, the Canadian capital, a gunman shot and killed Corporal Nathan Cirillo while he stood as an honorary guard at the National War Memorial. On December 2, 2015, in San Bernardino, California, a married couple shot and killed fourteen people. On June 12, 2016, a gunman opened fire in a nightclub in Orlando, Florida. At least forty-nine people were killed, and more than fifty were injured. This attack was the deadliest mass shooting in US history.

ISIS's campaign of hatred is focused on creating fear and division through acts of terror, such as the shootings in San Bernardino and Orlando. "Islamophobia" is a term used to describe a fear or hatred of Muslims. It is based on a stereotype that all Muslims are extremists who are violent toward non-Muslims. This misunderstanding helps further ISIS's goal of creating a rift between Muslims and non-Muslims that will rally more followers to its cause.

Spectators rush to help victims of the Boston Marathon bombing. The two brothers behind the attack were inspired by Islamic extremists.

I WITNESS WAR

Messages of love and tolerance are placed at a memorial for the victims of the Orlando nightclub shooting.

On December 6, 2016, at an air force base in Tampa, Florida, US President Barack Obama gave a speech outlining the country's plans to counter terrorism, both abroad and on US soil. He addressed the importance of standing united as one diverse country:

"If we stigmatize good, patriotic Muslims, that just feeds the terrorists' narrative. It fuels the same false grievances that they use to motivate people to kill. If we act like this is a war between the United States and Islam, we're not just going to lose more Americans to terrorist attacks, but we'll also lose sight of the very principles we claim to defend."

Why do you think the word "stigmatize" is used?

What is meant by the words "the terrorists' narrative"?

What principles do you think Obama is speaking about?

CHAPTER 6

FIGHTING BACK

In the early fight against ISIS, Iraqi and Syrian forces struggled on the battlefield against an unpredictable enemy. Today, a main focus of the Global Coalition is to train and arm the Iraqi army and Syrian opposition groups to defeat ISIS on the ground, to take back their homelands.

Once ISIS takes control of a city, it focuses on two areas: keeping civilians trapped inside and making it difficult for anyone to attack. To counter air strikes, ISIS lights fires on the oil fields it controls to make it difficult for pilots to spot their targets. The militants have also turned bomb-making into an industry. Entire factories dedicated to building bombs have been discovered in liberated areas. The militants use whatever materials they have on hand to build improvised explosive devices (IEDs). IEDs can be attached to cars or suicide vests, or hidden beneath the ground.

A German officer teaches a Peshmerga soldier how to search and disable IEDs.

Iraqi soldiers receive certificates after completing training provided by the US military in February 2017.

These homemade bombs can be triggered on contact or remotely, such as with an app on a smartphone. Coalition forces work closely with the Iraqi army to teach specialists how to detect and deactivate IEDs.

ISIS also digs extensive networks of tunnels beneath the cities its forces occupy. These tunnels allow fighters to move undetected and launch attacks on Coalition forces. Drones (unmanned robots) are used to scope out Coalition positions and drop bombs. One of the worst weapons ISIS uses to protect itself are innocent adults and children. In places such as Kobani, militants try to trap civilians inside the city to use as **human shields**. This makes it difficult for Coalition members to carry out air strikes when there is an added risk of civilian casualties.

To the west, in Syria, the complex web of different groups fighting in the Syrian civil war complicates the war against ISIS. The Syrian regime, led by Bashar al-Assad, is fighting the militants, while also battling rebel groups that oppose his leadership. The rebel groups opposing al-Assad are also fighting ISIS in different parts of the country. The two groups are supported by different countries. For example, Russia supports the al-Assad government, while the United States supports the rebel groups. Russia has carried out air strikes that target ISIS, as well as Syrian rebel forces.

In May 2015, Ramadi, the capital of Anbar province in Iraq, was captured by ISIS. In July, newly trained Iraqi troops began the fight to take back the city, and by December, they had driven out ISIS. This marked the first significant battle in which Iraqi troops had taken down an ISIS stronghold. With newfound momentum, the following summer, along with other forces and air support, they retook the nearby city of Fallujah, which had been under ISIS control for more than two years. As ISIS was driven out of Ramadi and Fallujah, the militants fell back to their stronghold in Mosul, 250 miles (400 km) away. When Iraqi troops entered Ramadi,

they found a city in ruin. More than six hundred air strikes had been made in the city and surrounding area. Mountains of rubble remained where buildings once stood. ISIS had also left the city booby-trapped with explosives. Bomb disposal teams worked to clear the streets to make it safe for civilians to return.

As the Coalition continued to push back IS in Iraq, the militants stepped up their acts of terror to pull attention away from the Coalition's momentum. In May 2015, IS captured the ancient city of Palmyra in central Syria. Over several months, many of the city's historic ruins were laced with explosives

Ramadi stands on the banks of the Euphrates River. During the ISIS occupation, the militants closed the dam, blocking the flow of water to towns and cities located downstream.

The Temple of Bel was one of the best-preserved structures in Palmyra. In 2015, ISIS blew up the temple. Only a single arch remains standing.

and destroyed, much to the shock of Syrians and the international community. In March 2016, Syrian government forces retook the city, but it fell again to ISIS in December of that same year. Today, almost all of Palmyra lies in utter ruin.

In 2015, ISIS released a video showing the destruction of artifacts in the Mosul Museum. Many of the museum's artifacts were from Nineveh, an ancient Mesopotamian site located near the city. Artifacts have also been looted, or stolen, and sold on the international black market. The money earned from these sales helps fund ISIS's terrorist activities. In efforts to safeguard their nations' cultural treasures, the governments of Syria and Iraq have made efforts to transport priceless artifacts to safer locations, away from the fighting.

On October 17, 2016, the Coalition and its partners launched an **offensive** to retake Mosul, the last ISIS stronghold in Iraq. On the battlefield, Iraqi and Kurdish forces gradually penetrated deeper into the city, with support from Coalition air strikes. After three months of fighting, Coalition forces secured parts of the city east of the Tigris River, which cuts through Mosul from north to south. As the troops grew closer, ISIS left obstacles built from rubble, wrecked cars, and shipping containers to slow the advance toward the city center. On January 24, the Iraqi prime minister, Haider al-Abadi, announced that eastern Mosul had been completely liberated. The fight, however, was not over; in western Mosul, about 750 thousand people remained trapped with limited access to food, water, and electricity.

A US convoy heads out to deliver supplies to Iraqi and Kurdish troops fighting on the front lines in Mosul.

I WITNESS WAR

Townsend became commander of the US-led Coalition in August 2016.

After eastern Mosul was liberated, Lieutenant General Stephen P. Townsend, the US commander of the Global Coalition, addressed the media. He spoke with admiration for the Iraqi military during the Mosul offensive:

"This is a monumental achievement for not only the Iraqi security forces and sovereign government of Iraq, but all Iraqi people. This would have been a difficult task for any army in the world. And to see how far the Iraqis have come since 2014, not only militarily, but in their ability to put their differences aside and focus on a common enemy, gives real hope to the people of Iraq that, after years of fighting and instability, peace and security are attainable. There is still a long way to go before ISIL is completely eliminated from Iraq, and the fight for western Mosul is likely to be even tougher than the eastern side. But the ISF [Iraqi Security Forces] have proven they are both a professional and formidable fighting force, and I have every confidence that ISIL's days are numbered in Iraq."

Why do you think the liberation of Mosul was a "monumental achievement" for all Iraqis?

The US military is the strongest in the world. Why is it significant that Townsend calls the fight against IS a "difficult task for any army in the world"?

What differences might the Iraqi forces have to put aside?

CHAPTER 7

COUNTERING HATE

The war against ISIS is not only being fought on the ground in Syria and Iraq. It is also being waged in the hearts and minds of people around the world.

Civilians are encouraged to report any profiles or posts that promote terrorism and extreme ideologies to social media companies.

For ISIS, social media is a powerful weapon. The group has been very effective at using sites such as Facebook to recruit and **radicalize** followers to its cause. People have traveled from all corners of the globe to join the caliphate. In December 2015, it was estimated that between twenty-seven thousand and thirty-one thousand people from at least eighty-six countries had gone to Syria and Iraq to join ISIS. Tunisia, Saudi Arabia, and Russia contributed the most jihadists. Many have also traveled from Western nations, including the United States, Canada, and the UK. Girls who travel to the caliphate are called "jihadi brides" because they go to marry ISIS fighters and have

children who will grow up to be ISIS soldiers. Once in the caliphate, many foreigners recruit more people from their native countries.

Homegrown terrorists have been inspired to launch attacks after watching **propaganda** videos posted by ISIS and other militant groups. The videos are professional and use violent imagery and twisted teachings of the Koran to convince people to join ISIS and travel to the caliphate. The group also publishes an online magazine called *Dabiq* in multiple languages, including English. The magazine is named after a small town in Syria near the Turkish border where ISIS militants believe they will fight their final battle against the enemies of their radical distortion of Islam.

The battle to counter ISIS's propaganda is being fought online. The US-led Coalition works to counter the militants' message of hate by sharing positive stories and information about people in the Middle East. Messages are posted in many languages, including Arabic, Urdu, Somali, and English. These are languages spoken in areas that the Coalition had identified as places ISIS may try and recruit followers. Social media companies such as Twitter and Facebook have also focused their efforts on shutting down accounts that promote terrorism. The online **activist** group, Anonymous, has also waged a cyber war against ISIS. In 2015, the group announced it had successfully taken down more than one thousand email and social media accounts and websites associated with ISIS.

The international community has responded in different ways to support the victims of the war against ISIS. In 2016, Canada granted **asylum** to four hundred Yazidi refugees, and in February 2017, the government promised to welcome 1,200 more. Germany has also accepted more than 1,100 Yazidi survivors. Twenty-five thousand Syrian refugees arrived in Canada in 2016. The United States settled 12,486 Syrians and 7,853 Iraqis. While it is important to support the victims of the war, some countries have also been hesitant to open their borders to Syrians and Iraqis. There is concern that as refugees flee to places such as Europe, ISIS soldiers will flee, too, disguised as victims rather than perpetrators of violence, and travel to foreign countries to launch deadly attacks. Many nations have tightened security and introduced intensive screening for people arriving from other countries.

On January 20, 2017, Donald Trump became the forty-fifth president of the United States. He campaigned on a promise to secure the United

Signs in English and Arabic welcome Syrian refugees to Toronto, Canada.

Protests have been held in cities around the world calling for people and governments to fight Islamophobia.

States' borders and defeat ISIS. A week after assuming the presidency, he issued an **executive order** that blocked people from seven Muslim-majority countries from entering the United States. The seven countries were identified as places where terrorist groups, including ISIS, operated. Syria and Iraq were both included, along with Iran, Libya, Somalia, Sudan, and Yemen. The ban was intended to protect against terrorist attacks on US soil. When the ban went into effect, there was chaos around the world. Citizens from the banned countries en route to the United States became stranded in airports. In major cities around the world

and across the United States, people staged protests against the ban, calling for the release of those who were detained. Many people thought that the ban reinforced ideas of Islamophobia. It was feared that targeting Muslim-majority countries would strengthen the idea that a war is being fought between the West and Muslims. Experts warned that this ideology could lead to recruits joining ISIS. News agencies reported that ISIS was celebrating the executive order, nicknaming it "the blessed ban." Several states challenged the order, and a federal judge suspended it. In March 2017, a revised document was released that removed Iraq—an important US ally in the battle against ISIS—from the ban.

People living in the war zones in Syria and Iraq continue to bear witness to the horrors of ISIS. They use social media to share their stories with the world. Raqqa is Being Slaughtered Silently (RBSS) is a group of Syrian activists based in Raqqa. They report information about human rights abuses at the hands of ISIS and the Syrian government. In the city, they work to counter the terrorists' message of hate with posters and graffiti. Members of RBSS risk their lives to share the truth about life inside the so-called capital of the caliphate.

By the end of 2016, the people of western Mosul had been imprisoned there for more than two years. In December, the Institute for War and Peace Reporting (IWPR), a UK-based charity, organized a letter-writing campaign to show support for the trapped Iraqis. Volunteers set up booths in different cities where people could write letters. More than two thousand letters were collected and then photocopied. On December 22, the Iraqi air force dropped four million letters from above the city, carrying messages of hope to the people trapped below.

The Iraqi air force carries out air strikes and also air-drops humanitarian aid to the innocent victims being held prisoner by ISIS.

I WITNESS WAR

An estimated 350 thousand children remained trapped in western Mosul in February 2017.

One letter from the Letters to Mosul campaign was written by a girl who signs her letter as the "daughter of Anbar." Her message reads:

"In the name of God the Merciful,
To our dear people, fathers, mothers, brothers, and sisters, we are with you in everything, and our hearts [go out] to you, and we feel what you feel of cold, hunger, and the harshness of days, and you should be patient and endured [assured] that victory is close, God willing ... Your sun will shine, and we will see the smile and joy on your faces and in the near [future], we will embrace each other and join each other and return Mosul to Iraq. Daughter of Anbar"

What words does the writer use to give hope to the people in Mosul?

What do you think she means by saying "your sun will shine"?

How does using the pronoun "we" instead of "I" affect her message?

43

In Syria, Coalition forces continue to advance toward Raqqa to take down the capital of the caliphate. In Iraq, the battle to liberate Mosul continues. The question of how destroyed cities will be rebuilt will undoubtedly shape the future of both Syria and Iraq. Raqqa is tied to the outcome of the Syrian civil war, which in 2017 entered its sixth year. The international community is also working with its allies in Syria and with the Iraqi government to plan long-term solutions to bring peace to this corner of the world.

Although the end may be within reach to defeat ISIS on the ground and dismantle its self-proclaimed

It will take many years to rebuild the cities and towns, such as Mosul, destroyed by the war against ISIS.

Members of the YPG and Syrian soldiers stand near the Euphrates River upstream from Raqqa, the last IS stronghold in Syria.

caliphate, the battle rages on to defeat its extremist ideologies that lead people to commit acts of terror all over the world. Some experts warn that even after the caliphate falls, ISIS will not be defeated. Its global arm now stretches beyond the Middle East, and its propaganda continues to inspire lone-wolf jihadists. There are also other terrorist organizations, such as Boko Haram and al-Qaeda, to combat in the larger War on Terror. When this chapter of world history closes, it will be remembered as a time when people of all faiths and nationalities came together to stand against an evil force that sought to divide, when stories of bravery were stronger than acts of terror, and when messages of love were stronger than messages of hate.

To learn more about the war against ISIS, write your own account of an event during this conflict.

1. Choose an event to focus your eyewitness account around, such as the liberation of Mosul or the Peshmerga rescue of the Yazidis from Mount Sinjar.

2. With an adult's help, find out more about your chosen event. Be careful when searching for information on the internet—some images and accounts of war can be graphic and disturbing. Discuss any questions and feelings you have about what you learn with a responsible adult.

3. Think about the perspective you will write your account from, such as a civilian, a soldier, or an aid worker.

4. Consider what form your eyewitness account will take. You can write a diary entry, blog post, or a letter. You could even send a reply to the letter on page 42, writing your response to the "daughter of Anbar."

GLOSSARY

activist A person who campaigns to bring about political or social change.

allegiance Loyalty or devotion.

asylum Protection granted by a state to someone who has left their country as a refugee.

autonomous Describing the right of a group or country to govern itself.

black market A system in which goods are purchased and sold illegally.

cells Small groups of between usually three to five terrorists.

civilians People who are not in the armed forces or police force.

civil war A war between organized groups in the same country.

coalition A group of people or countries that have joined together for a shared purpose.

crucifixions Executions by nailing people to a cross.

defector A person who deserts a cause.

dictator A ruler with total power over a country.

executive order An order made by the US president that is enforced as law.

hijab A headscarf worn by some Muslim women that covers their hair and neck.

humanitarian Concerned with preventing human suffering.

human shields People or a group of people held near a potential target to deter attack.

militants People who are aggressively involved in a cause.

niqab A full-body garment worn by some Muslim women that leaves only their eyes uncovered.

occupation Control of a foreign territory by armed forces.

offensive A large-scale military attack.

propaganda Information used to promote a particular point of view.

radicalize To have extreme beliefs on a subject, such as religion.

ransom Money paid to free someone who is held captive.

raped Forced, often violently, to have sex.

recruit To sign up new members.

sanctions Actions made to enforce rules or laws.

stigmatize To strongly disapprove of something or someone.

stronghold A place where a military group defends itself from attack.

suicide bombers People who commit suicide while setting off a bomb to kill other people.

Zoroastrianism An ancient religion based on the teachings of the prophet Zoroaster.

FURTHER READING

BOOKS

Kennan, Caroline. *The Rise of Isis: The Modern Age of Terrorism* (World History). Farmington Hills, MI: Lucent Press, 2017.

Marsico, Kate. *ISIS* (Special Reports). North Mankato, MN: ABDO, 2016.

Mooney, Carla. *Terrorism: Violence, Intimidation, and Solutions for Peace* (Inquire & Investigate). White River Junction, VT: Nomad Press, 2017.

Webb, Glenn. *Terrorism* (Critical World Issues). Broomall, PA: Mason Crest, 2017.

WEBSITES

CBC
http://www.cbc.ca/news/world/refugees-flee-isis-1.3235831
Refugees who have escaped from areas under ISIS control share their stories.

CNN
http://www. cnn.com/2014/08/08/world/isis-fast-facts
CNN provides a list of facts and links to articles on ISIS.

Global Coalition against Daesh
http://www. theglobalCoalition.org/en/partners
Visit the Global Coalition Against Daesh website to learn about international efforts to defeat ISIS.

UNICEF
http://www. unicef.org/infobycountry/iraq_74784.html
This UNICEF website focuses on the ongoing conflicts in Iraq and includes a list of articles about people affected by the war against ISIS.

INDEX

Acknowledgments:
The publisher would like to thank the following people for permission to use their material:
p. 9 Speckhard, Anne and Amhet S. Yayla. "Eyewitness Accounts from Recent Defectors from Islamic State: Why They Joined, What They Saw, Why They Quit." Perspectives on Terrorism, 2015. http://www.terrorismanalysts.com/pt/index.php/pot/article/view/475/html, p. 15 World Vision UK. "Children re-create war scenes in their first art class since fleeing Mosul." 2016. http://www.worldvision.org.uk/news-and-views/blog/2016/november/children-recreate-war-scenes, p. 21 Yazidi testimonial, CYCI, The Liberation of Christian and Yazidi Children of Iraq, p. 25 http://www.centcom.mil/operations-and-exercises/operation-inherent resolve/, Public domain: https://www.defense.gov/Resources/Privacy, p. 31 "Remarks by the President on the Administration's Approach to Counterterrorism." December 6, 2016. https://obamawhitehouse.archives.gov/the-press-office/2016/12/06/remarks-president-administrations-approach-counterterrorism, Public Domain: https://obamawhitehouse.archives.gov/copyright, p. 38 "Iraqi government announces liberation of Eastern Mosul." Department of Defense. January 24, 2017. http://www.centcom.mil/media/press-releases/Press-Release-View/Article/1058749/iraqi-government-announces-liberation-of-eastern-mosul, p. 42 "Iraqis air drop 'Letters to Mosul'" US Central Command, December 22, 2016. http://www.centcom.mil/media/press-releases/Press-Release-View/Article/1037057/iraqis-air-drop-letters-to-mosul/Public Domain: http://www.centcom.mil/Home/Privacy-and-Security/.